Goat on a Bike

Samantha Maw

Goat on a Bike

Copyright © Samantha Maw 2018

Illustrations by Laura Jones

ISBN-13: 978-1986432948

ISBN-10:1986432947

Contents

I

Poems to read to oneself whilst reclining in an armchair with a cuppa

*I used to live in Uganda and every day the strange
and unexpected would become my ordinary.
Returning to the UK, with its clear rules and
ingrained manners, was the real culture shock.*

Goat on a Bike

Goat on a bike
An undignified turkey
swinging
beady eyed
upended
feathers dancing
in the breeze
37 trays of eggs
on her head held
steady with a
scarred hand
A clutch of children
unbound behind a boda
grinning fearlessly in
in the heat soaked wind
A cackle of chickens
scattering like marbles
across the
orange dust
A confused tortoise
airborne like a trophy
The seller hoping for a good price
The product dreaming of lettuce
and a safe, warm box

A giant yellow bloom
of jerry cans banging
out a hollow tune
A woman walking
in her Sunday best
no shoes
A broad chested man
with a Hello Kitty Jacket
and a Santa hat
playing pool under a
hot tin roof
All traffic ignoring the red
lights and the Puffa fish
law enforcers in their white
jumpsuits and
oversized black boots
Armchairs stacked high
on a pick-up
a suited recliner enjoying
the wind on his face
The Blessed Furniture Centre
The Alleluia Tea Room Amen
This strangeness suits me
wraps around my soul
like I've returned home.

for ivan

i think of you often
as the sun licks the shadows off the hills
i think of your laughter
and how it shakes the morning
into the flurry of the day

i think of you under that blue white sky
treading through the sand, barefooted
a huge bright soul
wearing hope like a mantle

i note your bravery
pain hidden in soft lines
quoting broken english
with white chalk in your hair

i think of you often
when my sun dips
and yours is the song of the crickets
and we both make our way home...

musters road in spring

temporary bursts of soft pastel buds
short lived along musters road
a backdrop of blue listless cloud
moving over the city

a deceptively cold wind
marking my skin with long fingers
etching its final comment
across the fading winter sky

snowdrops standing strong against frost and winds
listening out for the first signs of spring
conversation reverts to signs of the season
and my heart feels bright with change

A Joik for all Seasons

He said there was a Joik for all seasons,
for every creature plant and tree.
for the sky, the skimming clouds,
the sea.
He spoke with soft caressing tones
and feint melodic moans and
his fingers were butterflies
dancing.
I wasn't sure what a Joik was but
I didn't much care
I was hypnotised by his
incandescent stare,
the movement of his lips,
the penetrating rhythm of his hips.

He handled the crowd with ease
and when he asked me to
rustle his leaves
I was happy to assist.
I crushed them like eggshells
in my fist.

Night time conversation

Describe it to me, you said.

The first time was tender,
intense and surprising.
It broke my spirit.

The second was sweet,
sensuous and smacked of stability.
It scared me to death.

The third was raw,
reckless and hard to resist.
It blew open my soul.

But which one was real you asked.
Perhaps all of them I said.
Perhaps none at all.

Try again you said.
Perhaps not I thought.
Noting the space in my heart
between the first and the last.

Definitely Autumn

Definitely Autumn

as the west wind spins our path to gold

whipping hair and skin and sensibilities

starch sky behind us like a backdrop

Jess enveloped in spiralling leaves and

springing in the gathering plume

remember this moment

this air

this sky

this dying amber light

turning

us

both

into

shadows

Poetry in Progress

You talked of poetry in progress,
You, with your sea green eyes
and your soft smile.
And there was me
(not wanting to seem pretentious)
trying to put what I had learnt into words.

You talked of love
in progress like a poem.
My blue green eyes
Lingering.
Turning you over.
Chasing possibility.

*On September 19th, 1942, my Grandfather set out
with five other Wimpeys to attack Tobruk. His
plane was shot down over the desert and
miraculously, he survived. I have taken the words
from his own recount and rearranged them in a
poem.*

Shot down over Tobruk

The starboard spluttered
Jettisoned; lost height.
I had seen the others go
and abandoned myself,
plummeted out facing the
tail 800 feet to the ground,
swivelling rapidly like
a joint on a spit.

I hit the ground
before I was ready,
wondering a hundred things,
my period of recovery
shortened by a distant thud.
The old familiar flames,
the pall of black smoke.

All were raw -
I thought, new to the desert,
hardly knew North from South
by the stars.
Limping in the half moon light

among rocks and uneven ground,
taking bearings by the moon
descending into deep, dry wadis;
finally falling by the port wings.
I dozed in the bitter damp
until dawn but couldn't sleep.
I couldn't verify the North Star.
I couldn't figure out the plough.
Hour by hour,
I pieced them together.

As soon as light broke I plundered
the wreckage.
A splint for my leg,
a dural tube,
Horlicks tablets and a
pint of water, my note
for safe passage, first aid.
Liberia traced on silk,
half a parachute,
and my pistol.

I walked, hobbled, hid
from the heat
a colossal distance,
parachute wrapped turban like,
and at mid-day draped
over a thorn bush for shade.
Swollen and bruised I slept,
and the hands on my watch stood still.

A sea breeze blew by day
(It was North
 but had some West)
then damn nearly a full moon
and the Sea itself! But believe
nothing that you think you see.
Only rocks.
The next rise in the ground.

4 or 5 marches from
a line of barren hills,
I sank into the smooth sand,
depleted.
Close to the coast road,
I gave myself up to the
hum of a Schwimmwagen
and a Mauser Automatic.

Big Questions

`What is heaven like? `
She asks with confusion
etched on her young face
(she has had her hand up for a while).
Every time I pass her by,
she crinkles her brow
then lifts herself
higher in her seat.
I have told them to ask
Big Questions,
hoping some will find the answers.
`Heaven?
It's a place where good people go, `
he says confidently, with a nod.
Like it's a fact.
Eleven years young
and contemplating life
behind a blue topped table
with a stub of pencil.

Where have you been?

Where have you been?
the carved steel questions,
as I take refuge under its arches.
Not a question for me but
for the darkening river beneath.

I have passed by often,
seen the changing facades.
Framing the progress of time.
But you have always been here-
your sinews streaming
past harried steps.

Mesolithic man amassing near your banks,
the Corieltauvi settlement seeking refuge.
The Romans arriving in triumph,
the Britons taking territory.
The Anglo Saxons revering their dead,
The Vikings sailing their ships.
Conquering William forcing passage,
a fortress built, a great house of God,
the sainted monks praying and
a mercenary King.

All that and now me,
heading softly into the unravelling gloom.

II
Poems to read aloud to
your friends after a glass of
wine (or two)

There's Something about Frank

There's something about Frank
that leaves me wanting more,
I can smell him from a mile away-
we're meant to be I'm sure.

I see him in the distance
and my heart begins to race,
It's simply Frank and Frank alone
that stirs my happy place.

There he is! Oh, there he is!!
I start to fantasise
about his manly jawline
and his sturdy well-built thighs.

His golden coat is shining
as he sniffs and marks his spot.
I'm not concerned with other boys
It's Frank that makes me hot.

He's spotted me- he's turned around,
his tail has started swishing!
Oh, Frank please say you feel the same-
I'm dog- tired of just wishing.

You're all I ever wanted and
you're such a charming mutt.
If you play your cards right Frank,
I'll let you sniff my butt.

Song for a Yeller Belly

Edith's face were harrowed
as she looked at husband Jack,
"There's nowt I like about that sky,
It's looking rare and black."

Farmer Jack were proper frit of
tatey harvest failing,
the breedlings, they were chuntering
and one or two were ailing.

The siling rain had done its wurst,
the snithe wind made them keel,
Jack's fizzog weren't a pretty sight
-enough to make ya beel!

Feeling arsey varsey and as
mardy as his bum,
He heard his wife say, "Cheer up Duck,
There's better things to come!"

Rik the Kitchen Fitter

Rik the kitchen fitter
is really quite a man.
If anyone can make the earth move,
Rik the fitter can.

He stands out from the other guys
at a lofty six foot two.
And when you greet him on the street,
he'll always smile at you.

He has a build like Sly Stallone,
He's used to heavy lifting.
He's useful for installing pipes
or cupboards that need shifting.

When Rik the fitter rings the bell,
my knees both turn to jelly.
He's far more entertaining than
Loose Women on the tele.

He's here till Spring, my husband says
He could have finished sooner,
but I don`t mind him coming `round
And nor does my dog Luna.

When she sees him in his yellow van,
she can't contain her glee;
she puts her paws up on his lap
and shares his builder`s tea.

Oh! How I wish my Fred was like
that Rik, the kitchen fitter.
I'll miss him when he's done the job,
But search for him on twitter.

For Lucy and Luna

My Cat Flap
(not a euphemism)

I'm tired of letting them in and out
all hours of the day.
They need more independence
 I can hear my neighbour say.
"Get one of those posh cat flaps
that stops others getting in,
that microchip technology's
the very latest thing."
Now with all things technological,
I'm a little cautious,
and the thought of spending extra cash,
makes me feel quite nauseous.
But I took the plunge, I took a risk,
I got a friend to fit it,
when it comes to DIY,
I'm proper clueless, I'll admit it.
After several hours of dust and that
incessant heavy drilling,
the cat flap sat proudly inside
the large hole it was filling.
Now the time had come
for battery insertion,
the cats were not impressed at their
unsightly door conversion.
I tried to get them through the hole
to register their chip,
Gracie squeezed her bottom through,
but Georgie didn't fit.

The red light kept on flashing,
an error was displayed,
then the door refused to close
and I regretted that I'd paid
for this piece of fancy kit
that was letting all the rain in.
I would have to call the company
and waste my time explaining
why it wasn't working,
after following instructions,
and if I didn't get a refund,
there would certainly be ructions!
My cats now sit there quite bemused
each side of the clear plastic,
and I want to punch my neighbour
when she says my flap's fantastic.

The Birds, the Beasts and the Bat
An Aesop's Fable

There was a time long ago,
when all was not well,
and the birds and the beasts planned to fight.
They didn't feel like sharing the land; and
met in the woods one dark night.

The armies stood strong
on opposite sides,
with fearful looks on their faces.
"Please wait!" said the bat as he looked back and
forth
"First let me find where my place is!"

"Choose us," sang the Birds
"We'll attack from above,
we have sharp beaks and we're very clever."
"But I am no bird!" the little bat cried,
"I'm a beast and I will be for ever."

"Choose us!" growled the Beasts
"We have strength on our side,
And with sharp teeth our foe will die quickly,"
"I'm a bird!" said the bat as he dithered and dived,
And felt rather nervous and sickly.

After thought and repose,
the animals chose to
live peacefully, all with one voice,
"What a wonderful outcome!" the little bat said,

"Now with whom should I sing and rejoice?"
"Not with us!" sang the Birds,
and they all flew away,
so he tried to make friends with the Beasties.
They chased him as far as the edge of the wood;
"Come back and we'll tear you to pieces!"

The little bat flew
alone through the world.
He should have just made a decision.
Choose whom you serve and then stand by their side,
 if you want to escape such derision.

Happy Ever After

You're not the one I wanted.
You have pimples on your chin.
Your hair is thinning badly,
And your legs are way too thin.

You're not the one I wanted.
You're too saggy round the middle.
It really puts me off when I
want to have a fiddle.

You're not the one I wanted.
MUST LIKE DOGS the advert said.
You smell like one and I am loath
to have you in my bed.

You're not the one I wanted.
Your snoring drives me crazy!
I wake up like Frankenstein;
while you're fresh as a daisy

You're not the one I wanted.
You always want to rest.
You would prefer to stay at home
and balance beer on your chest.

You're not the one I wanted.
You leave toenails in the bath.
And when I start to have a go-
you leg it down the path.

You're not the one I wanted.
But when you asked me for a dance,
I was taken by your charming smile
and thoughts of true romance.

You're not the one I wanted.
You don't look like Cary Grant.
And I know that I'm no Doris Day,
so please excuse the rant.

You're not the one I wanted.
But you're mine in all your glory.
I'm not the one you wanted,
but we're here to tell the story!

Poo Bag in a Tree

Oh, poo bag

swinging on your

high perch

moonlight caressing your

unsanitary curves

making your home amongst

the crows

blending into the

dark secrets of the night

Oh, poo bag

what crosses your

mind

as you hang with

malevolence

surveying the

hurried steps

of

harangued humanity

you have escaped the

deadly confines

of the

poo bin

where you might have

suffocated between

the

plethora of faecal matter

yours was a different path

you were raised up from the
doggy detritus from which you were
birthed to feel the wind at your back
and the world beneath your feet

as I gaze up at you and your entourage
of ageless stars it causes me to ponder
the very nature of
our fleeting existence and ask:

*"What moron
threw that up there?"*

There's a Lizard in my Bra

There's a Lizard in my bra,
there's a cockroach in my pants.
There are rats in my back passage
and my bed is full of ants.
I am running out of gas -
it's ten miles to the garage.
On the way, I'm offered cows;
and a tempting arranged marriage.
The traffic cops have stopped me,
hoping it's their lucky day.
If I offer them a soda, then
they'll send me on my way.
My suspension is collapsing
due to large holes in the road
and the traffic rules are hard to read-
forget the highway code!
There are goats too near my bumper,
there are chickens on the path
there are Boda-Bodas streaming past;
they just look at me and laugh.

Africa, you have my heart-
my digestive system too,
despite the plate sized spiders
and surviving gastric flu.

Song for a Supply Teacher

Those who can't do tend to teach,
 or so the saying goes.
Those who can't teach do supply,
you're thinking that, I know.
But could you get up with the birds
– sit waiting for that call,
Teacher`s toolkit by your side,
an activity for all?
Would you be prepared to travel
somewhere different every time?
And although you're left no planning,
say, "It`s completely fine!"

Could you process all procedures
within seconds of arrival?
All the things you need to know
that are key to your survival?
Like, where to find the workbooks
and when Jimmy takes his meds?
And that Ellen is allergic to
every type of bread?
Could you learn a bunch of names,
just by looking at their faces?
Could you locate all the missing shoes
and know where each child's place is?

Could you troubleshoot the I.C.T
and improv when it fails?
Restore some equilibrium

when anarchy prevails?
Could you feed the classroom gerbil
and teach it long division?
Show how to use a modal verb,
then make a prompt decision
on how to extract Reece
from underneath the table -
get him to drop the kitchen knife
before he grows unstable?

Talk about the sex life of a
flower bearing tree?
Slip into some football shorts
and be a referee?
Demonstrate gymnastic poses,
lead an action song?
Make a pouch for Sarah's tooth
and smile all day long?
Be on speaking terms with
a non-English speaking child?
Cut out laminated letters;
stop the fish from being defiled?

Deal with fist fights on the playground,
Clean the vomit from your shoes?
Talk of making the right choices,
Make them all line up in twos?
Could you fill out all the forms
and type up all the letters?
Mark a hundred books knowing
that Miss Bailey does it better?

Could you do it all again in
a different place each day,
without a mental breakdown
 and the urge to run away?

Those who can't do tend to teach?
You'd better not mean me?
We are TEACHING SUPERHEROES

and I'd like to see you do it.

A legacy of words

I want to leave

a legacy of words.

To be heard. My

life transferred.

Not a plea for fame,

but a hope that my

name will remain -

at least on a page.

My presence noted

in the vast swell

of time. A sign

I was once here.

And that these

marks

were

mine.

Samantha Maw has recently completed her MA in Creative Writing at the University of Lincoln (England.). She is a member of Lincoln Creative Writers, Women in the Arts Lincoln, and Outspoken Poets. She regularly performs at local and national Spoken Word events and writes for The Blue Nib Literary Journal.

Find her on Facebook and Twitter

Check out her blog at www.couragechasers.com

16121031R00023

Printed in Great Britain
by Amazon